Successful
Potty
Training

Also available in the NANNY KNOWS BEST series
Easy Weaning & First Feeding
Stop Your Baby's Crying
Coping with Temper Tantrums

Successful Potty Training

Nanny Smith

with Nina Grunfeld

VERMILION
LONDON

First published in 1996

1 3 5 7 9 10 8 6 4 2

First published in the United Kingdom in 1996
by Vermilion, an imprint of Ebury Press,
Random House, 20 Vauxhall Bridge Road,
London SW1V 2SA

Random House Australia (Pty) Limited
20 Alfred Street, Milsons Point, Sydney
New South Wales 2061, Australia

Random House New Zealand Limited
18 Poland Road, Glenfield
Auckland 10, New Zealand

Random House South Africa (Pty) Limited
PO BOX 337, Bergvlei, South Africa

Random House UK Limited Reg. No. 954009

A CIP catalogue record for this book is available from the
British Library.

ISBN: 0 09 180940 1

Printed and bound in Great Britain by
Mackays of Chatham plc, Kent

CONTENTS

AUTHOR'S NOTE

Unless a specific child is being written about, throughout the book your baby is refered to as 'he', not because of any bias but to differentiate you, the mother or child carer, from your baby.

Also, the term 'potty training' has been used throughout instead of 'toilet training' as that is the term we always used. It covers lavatory training too.

CHAPTER ONE

Be Positive

THIS BOOK IS ABOUT ATTITUDES – YOURS, NOT YOUR child's. To make your life easy and keep your child happy it is so important to have the correct approach to potty training. Even if you have had problems the first time you tried to potty train your child, you can now try again using my easy approach and a calm attitude. To help your child you have to be methodical, patient, relaxed and *on his side*.

Why you feel as you do

I think that often trouble is caused by well-meaning friends and family questioning what parents are doing and offering advice. This confuses the parent, undermines their confidence and can lead to the parent feeling inadequate and fearful, which in turn reflects on the child. People also like to compare their children with yours, theirs always favourably, of course. They will have stories about how very quickly their children were potty trained – stories which are probably grossly exaggerated. Those sort of remarks are best ignored; it is an extraordinary thing to show off about.

Another difficulty with potty training is, I think, that hidden deep down there is a slightly sad feeling that the last vestige of babyhood has gone with the end of the nappy. One should really feel so pleased that it is not so time consuming and so much easier in various ways, but at the same time it is a sad that he is one step forward to being an adult and the little tiny person that has relied on you for food and nappies and transport is becoming increasingly independent. These feelings of wanting the child to be dependent and yet independent can be confusing for the child and may cause problems.

It won't last for ever

The emotion parents feel so often, especially with a first child, is that most steps in bringing up a child are never going to end. You think your child is never going to stop spitting out food or waking up in the night, yet if you look back over the past few months you will realise what a lot has already been achieved. Feeling impatient only puts pressure on your child about something that really doesn't matter.

At the moment it is impossible for you to imagine that one day your child will be going to the lavatory like anybody else. It seems to be taking weeks, even months to train him, and you can't quite believe that within a relatively short time this so-called problem will be behind you.

Potty training is one of the areas that most distresses parents and yet, even if you stopped training your child tomorrow, he would not be going off to school wearing nappies. He would have control of his bladder, control of his bowels and would sooner or later, if he had the chance to see other people use the lavatory, be using it too. Yet leaving a child to his own devices would be a comparatively lengthy and anti-social business and so your job is to gently encourage him to use a pot for everyone's sake. Remember that potty training is not about training the child when and how to defecate, but *where*. It is about encouraging the child to deposit his waste products in a certain place.

Before we can choose from the options available to us to achieve this, we need to see the training process in relation to the child's abilities and understand his point of view.

How Potty Training Works

There are three stages to potty training: forming a habit, gaining control and then having results.

Forming a habit

The first stage really has nothing to do with the child's urine or faeces and where and when to empty them. The idea behind this first stage is really just to help the child experience sitting on a pot and getting used to a regular routine of sitting on it, which is why it is so important to have a comfortable one. So that when the time does come for the child to understand the purpose of using the pot he is as used to sitting on it as he is to having a bath.

Sitting a child on a pot at regular times to form the habit is not to condition him to use it. You can't condition a one-year-old child to open his bowels at certain times because a child, like an adult, can only open his bowels when his insides are ready. Just as you can sometimes do a pee 'on demand' if you need to go out, so a child can on occasions be induced to pass water (old fashioned nannies, if they wanted the child to spend a penny before they were going out to the park, would blow on the child's bottom to make them urinate). But you can never open your bowels on demand and nor can your child.

Gaining control

The second stage of potty training you don't need to teach – and indeed, you can't teach. It is when a child realises that his body is telling him something and that something could be that he needs to urinate, or it could be that he needs to defecate. These two feelings ('bladder control' and 'bowel control') don't necessarily happen at the same time. Children usually get bowel control first, but it can be the other way round. Bladder and bowel control usually happen between eighteen months and two and a half years, although with boys it may be three years.

Having results

The third stage of potty training is when a child can associate the feelings he has in his bladder and bowels with the substances he sees in the pot. This is so much easier for a child if he has been sitting on a pot for a while and is therefore familiar with the substances he has seen in the pot. If you try to introduce a pot to a child only after he has got bladder and bowel control he may resent having to interrupt his play to sit on a pot or lavatory – after all, it's so much easier (and warmer) to wee (or poo) in your pants and play at the same time. If your child has been sitting on the pot for a while he will by now have understood why and the whole thing will have fallen into place.

When to start?

Nine months is the best age to first put the child on the pot because children are getting a little bit more aware by then and the pot is comfortable and fun. They can generally sit up, they enjoy swinging their legs whilst sitting on the pot, and it is something else to do when they aren't yet usually crawling about much. Also, as most babies just defecate once a day at this age (usually after breakfast), if you catch something in the pot as well then that is useful, because you don't have so many bottoms and nappies to wash. You could start at a year, but one would never start at six months because they wouldn't be able to sit up by themselves.

The snags of starting late

These days the fashion is to put off introducing a child to a pot until the child wishes to sit on it or until you think he wishes to sit on it. This can result in children not accepting the idea of sitting on the pot for a considerable time, although I have known mothers who have trained their two and a half year old children in one day just by letting them run around in the garden without pants on. It worked for them but it had meant six months more of washing nappies (or buying them, which is expensive), six months more of washing bottoms, six months more of unpleasant nappies for other people to smell and, lastly, using a system which may work for some but not for others.

A rebel without a cause

I've heard people say that the danger of starting early is that once the child begins to understand what he is doing and has control of his bladder and bowels he may decide not to co-operate and you have to start again. In other words that by introducing the pot early you are giving him something else to oppose, something else to rebel against. But rebellion is part of childhood and one of your skills as a parent or keeper is to make all the stages of childhood comfortable and happy and to see that if a child wants to rebel you remove the cause of his rebellion. Whether you start early or late the child may rebel against the pot at some stage, but it is not the pot that causes rebellion.

Certainly, when started early, the pot is something they know about and if they rebel you just introduce it again. If they start late it is something very alien in their lives and they may well not want to use it. It seems unkind to try and insist that they use it when it is something that has never been in their lives before. I also think that a parent starting late expects a bit more from their child, that their child will co-operate and sit on the pot and that if the child doesn't want to it may just set up a tiny area of conflict between parent and child. People lead busy lives and a parent who has a child who doesn't seem interested in using the pot, jumps up the moment he is put on it, or who refuses to sit on it, can find this frustrating, especially if she has to stop what she is doing to clean the mess up.

Picking your time

Because childcare is supposed to be instinctive, most people have had no training in how to care for them. Of course the maternal instinct is directed towards preservation, so babies are taken great care of, but as time passes the approach to feeding and potty training and so on can present lots of problems because there are so many different ways of handling the various stages. All things pass and everything always works out well in the end but I often feel that it would have saved a lot of anxiety on the mother's part if various simple rules and approaches could have been known to them.

Theories about potty training change all the time. I knew a few nannies who used to perch a brand new baby on a soap dish or a very small pot in order that he weed. It was, of course, ludicrous as little babies empty their bladders very, very frequently and so even if the baby did wee in the soap dish, a few minutes later he would do it again in his nappy. At that age urinating is automatic – when the bladder is full, it empties itself.

Today the tendency is equally extreme the other way, with two-year-old babies making a very smelly, anti-social situation for other people and I have even heard mothers complaining that it is difficult to find nappies large enough for their four-year-old to wear at night. Although it may only take a day to teach a child to use the lavatory it is a risk. With an older child there are far more likely to be battles of wills and, as you know, battling with a child over anything at all can only make you the loser.

Another disadvantage about leaving potty training until the child is older is that you may have the worry of a nursery school or playgroup that wants your child to be potty trained before he attends. If so, find one that doesn't mind your child being in nappies or, best of all, keep him at home. Adding an external pressure to potty training may well make it worse for both of you.

I was once asked about a child who was three and a half and would only defecate if a nappy was put on her. Her parents were worried that she would not be accepted for school if it was not solved.

I told them to get rid of the nappies and introduce her to sitting on the lavatory with a child's seat and footstool (see Chapter Three). However, the most important thing was for them to forget about school as it was adding an extra pressure to their lives and one which was not necessary as she would be out of nappies very soon. I told them never to say to their daughter 'They won't allow you to go to school if you still wear nappies' as as children do understand so much more than people realise and she might well be thinking 'I needn't go to whatever this school is if I don't use the pot'. (See also Chapter Seven.)

The Easy Way

I consider my way of potty training children, which I explain fully in Chapter Four, to be a happy medium. By starting quite early I never have a battle. Even if the child rebels and doesn't want to sit on his pot then I never make him, but my way of potty training is such a slow, gradual process that there is no need to rebel. Also, starting when the child is so young avoids any frustrations – it's not as if he wants to go out and play with his friends.

Underlying my whole approach to potty training are my Four Golden Rules (see Chapter Two). It's essential to read this chapter first, whether you choose to train your child The Easy Way, early on, or a little later.

The Four Golden Rules
are as follows:

1 Children have no natural shame about their bodily functions (unless you make them ashamed).

✦

2 Children need routine (not rewards).

✦

3 Children don't want to talk about potty training (and you shouldn't either).

✦

4 Every child is an individual whose rights and feelings should be respected.

CHAPTER TWO

Four Golden Rules

THESE FOUR GOLDEN RULES ARE ABOUT THE WAY you should approach potty training – and your child – at whatever age you have chosen to start training. Most of my worries come from first time parents who are concerned about the job in hand; a second child is usually much happier than a first to sit on the pot. He has an older example to follow and a parent who has seen it all before and is usually more relaxed. This doesn't mean that I never hear potty training problems from parents of second or third children – far from it – I do.

The first Golden Rule:
✦ Children have no natural shame about their bodily functions (unless you make them ashamed).

Children learn by copying

When they are very small, children copy everything and quite often you don't realise a nervous mannerism you have until you see your child trying to copy what he has seen you do. They get into an awful muddle but they want to do it too. Early on in their lives, everything they do is learnt by copying and it is noticeable in the games children play. For instance, when they play with a little tea set, pouring out the tea and pretending to pour the milk in, just as they have seen you do. Therefore if there is a relaxed attitude in the family towards sitting on the lavatory, it doesn't necessarily mean that they will want to copy that – at least not until they are two or two and a half – but it does mean they have always seen it happen and they won't query why they themselves are being put on a pot or lavatory.

Be a little casual

Of course, your child doesn't have to see you on the lavatory if you would rather he didn't, but if it can be something that you are relaxed about – leaving the door open, for example, so that you don't shut your child out – it will indicate that going to the lavatory is not something to be worried about. If every time you go to the bathroom and shut and lock the door behind you, you are shutting the child out – I have known children kick and scream and shout when they are being excluded. Those children are also now potty trained and happily using the lavatory (possibly also now shutting and locking the door) but it is an attitude that could add to the stress of potty training whilst it is going on.

A certain amount of modesty is not to be derided, but if people can be relaxed about their children seeing them undressed or bathing or going to the loo children will just accept it. Being a little casual is a healthy attitude to have. I have come across quite small children who have closed the door to go to the loo or to get dressed, or who say 'Don't look' as they are taking off their night-wear and putting on their clothes for the day. This excessive modesty is learnt behaviour. It makes for a much more relaxed and mentally happy child if these things are not hidden away.

How copying helps later on

You can use copying to your advantage in later potty training. Before going out for a walk children often say they don't want to go to the loo, but if you say 'I'm going, come and keep me company' and sit on the loo to spend your penny and sit the child on the pot next to you, you will very often find he does the same. The sound of the running water very often encourages the child to do it in the pot. This could almost be a routine, before meals, or going shopping, or going for a walk, both of you going to the loo at the same time – 'I'm popping, are you?' Your child might even pretend he's popping to copy you.

You may also notice later in potty training that a girl child very often tries to copy a boy child standing up to wee. The little girl stands up to wee and, of course, it goes all down her legs. A very small girl doesn't realise that it's because the boy has a 'handy gadget' (as one little girl remarked about her brother's willy) that he can do it and she can't. If your daughter stands up and wees I would just say 'Let's get some clean pants.' I wouldn't say 'Don't try it again!' because she will have realised that it doesn't work. If she asks 'How does Tommy do it?' I would just explain that he is a little boy and has a different sort of botty.

Children also copy disgust

Children who haven't yet been conditioned to be disgusted by excreta are very often fascinated by it and want to peer into the pot, once they have got off it, and look ever so closely to see what they have done – very often their noses almost touch it they are so intrigued. Small children left longer than necessary on their own, either on the pot or in bed in the morning, often play with their excreta, smearing it over themselves and around the cot and walls. They are bored and seeking attention. I wouldn't tell them off, just clean it up and try not to leave them on their own for long periods of time.

Childish smut

Of course, no matter how relaxed you are, your child will eventually come home from school and say 'Poo-poo' and 'willy' and giggle a lot and tell you disgusting rhymes. Once children start school most of them start talking about it and giggling about it, some more than others, but they do all influence each other. The thing to do is completely ignore it and if they enlarge upon it, just say 'Why do you think it's funny?' not aggressively, keep it light-hearted. If they reply 'Well, Johnny told it to me', just calmly reply 'What a funny thing to say.' Once they realise that they can't get a rise out of you by repeating their lavatory humour they will soon not bother to say it.

The same goes for lavatory swearing. If they say 'You're a smelly poo-poo' or 'You've got a big bum', again I would not take any notice. If your children keep taunting each other with these expressions I would say 'Doesn't James say silly things, his poo-poo is smelly too', but if possible I would try not to get involved. I would be a little firm with the taunter if it is upsetting the taunted. If you can, just keep calm and divert their attention with a brisk 'Who's going to get into the bath first?'

Try not to show your revulsion

I think children only become obsessed with excreta if people laugh and talk about it. After all, excreting is a perfectly normal thing to do, it is essential for living, and even though the subject of both excreta and urine is still considered taboo by many people, it is important that your attitude to your child's natural bodily functions should not show or express any disgust at all or this could cause problems with potty training.

I was once told by a woman that the first time her twenty-six-month-old daughter had done a poo in the pot the child was quite frightened and has refused to use the potty or the lavatory ever since. I said I could imagine that a child of this age, never having seen a bowel movement before, could be quite disturbed by it, because with a nappy it is cleaned up and wiped off and looks different – so she would not have related the two things. However, what struck me most, was the mother's avoidance of the word 'excreta' or 'bowel movement' or 'poo'. Instead, throughout our entire conversation, she referred to 'it' and 'the other requirement'. My feeling was that instead of saying to her daughter 'Oooh, look. Aren't you clever. Look what you've done. Well done, you', she had probably expressed some of the disgust that she felt.

The child was now two and a half and put into a nappy for her bowel movements. I told the mother that she should dispose of the nappies and simply wear little pants. I explained that she would initially try not to empty her bowels as the nappy was no longer there but would eventually do it in her pants. At this point the mother shouldn't scold or make any remark other than 'Let's go and put some clean ones on' and after breakfast just suggest 'Let's go to the pot now. Would you like to try and do it in the pot? It's a good time to do it after breakfast'. I advised the mother not to talk about it or make a fuss and in a couple of weeks the child should be doing it in the pot. The mother should be able to tell when her daughter needed the pot and could then read her a story, or talk to her, to get her (and her mother) to relax, and then the daughter should be praised if she succeeded.

I also suggested that she found a word that she was happy with to use for talking about her child's bowel movements. When I was a child we always used to call it 'Number Two' ('Number One' being urine) or 'Big Job', but now 'Poo' seems to be the accepted name for it.

I have met other people who were very concerned and annoyed because a child occasionally defecated in her pants and I've pointed out that if the bowels were not emptied the child would die – after all, you've got to get rid of waste products. I suggested to one such mother that she should try to remember that her daughter *had* to empty her bowels and it wouldn't take long before she could do it in the loo by herself. It certainly is a great nuisance if a child defecates in his pants, especially if out shopping or visiting friends or relations or at any busy moment in your day. But it really doesn't take that long to deal with and it is just a passing phase. People feel that babies are never going to walk, never going to talk, never going to sleep – all things pass. If the mother can just be relaxed about it it will help both her and her child. She should tell herself that it won't go on forever. It certainly should not become a big issue – not a topic of conversation over dinner. (See also the third Golden Rule.)

I have heard people say 'Oh, what a stinky nappy!' or 'What a dirty bottom!' to a two-year-old who is still wearing nappies. It must somehow make the child feel they have done something wrong and yet the nappy has been put on the child to use. I don't agree with this business of leaving nappies on children until they were two and three, but do try never to show any disgust when peeling off a soiled one. If you don't want the nappy to be soiled, don't put it on. By two years a child is usually perfectly capable of being without a nappy.

'Accidents' due to misunder- standings

Even a potty trained child can be held back by a parent or keeper expressing revulsion. If a child has what is referred to as an 'accident' in his pants it is essential not to scold the child and not to show disgust but to say calmly 'Let's go upstairs and find some more panties.' Then stand him in the bath, peel his pants off, wash his bottom and find him some new pants. This must be your attitude throughout. To him, wetting or soiling his pants is not a problem and he will accept you changing his pants and hosing him down and won't think 'I shouldn't have done that because it's dirty.'

When people show disgust or anger when a small child fills his pants with poo or urine, their reaction does instil a certain fear into a child – not a fear of doing it into his pants but a fear of doing it at all. He doesn't understand that you are angry about the pants, he thinks you are angry because he has had a bowel movement so he might well not use the pot when you sit him on it because he thinks you don't want him to use it. I have known children doing it in their pants and then running away because they are afraid of being scolded for doing it, thus dirtying pants becomes a sort of a sin – a crime almost, although sometimes, if they've had a lot of fruit, say, they simply can't help it.

Treat such accidents light-heartedly. Even if you tell him 'Sweetie, don't do it in your pants, do it in the pot' he won't quite know what you mean. Don't worry that you're going to upset your child for life if you show a little annoyance, because you probably are very, very busy and you'd really rather it hadn't happened, just try not to be aggressive. You could say something along the lines of: 'Oh, what a nuisance, what a bore. Just hang on whilst I finish this and then we'll go upstairs and make a nice, clean botty.' They're probably feeling uncomfortable enough about having wet or soiled pants without any further recriminations to make them feel guilty.

A mother once told me about her four-year-old son who regularly did little bits of poo in his pants. He never asked to go to the loo, but she said that she knew when he needed to defecate because she could either smell something or she would see him disappearing behind a piece of furniture. When she then put him on the loo he would do a poo but this only happened every two or three days. She thought that the reason he used his pants rather than the loo was that he was lazy and it made her go completely 'bonkers'.

I found this an incredibly complicated situation which was getting worse. It might have started during potty training with the child soiling his pants and being scolded. Since then he had started hanging on to his poo. I explained that far from being lazy her son was waiting as long as he could before he defecated because to him defecation was a sort of a crime which he was anxious to avoid. On the other hand he also now needed the attention that his soiled pants produced and was reluctant to give that up.

I suggested she sought medical advice to reassure herself that there was nothing amiss and bought her son a large chamber pot to use instead of the loo. She should casually invite him to use it after breakfast, saying something like 'Come and sit on his nice big pot for ten minutes and see if you can do a poo. I'll read you a story or perhaps you'd rather look at the book yourself? If you could do a poo in there it will save all that bother having to change your pants.' After a while she wouldn't have to sit with him any more, it would be part of his routine.

✦ Remember: Children have no natural shame about their bodily functions (unless you make them ashamed).

Children Need Routine

For a child's well-being and sense of security, routine is essential. This is not to say that one has to be hidebound about it, but keep to a regular daily regime as far as possible. For routine leads to a child feeling that everything is alright and he doesn't really have to question anything. Of course occasionally plans have to be changed for various reasons, but there shouldn't be a great fuss made about it.

By and large a small child's life should be the same. This applies to all aspects of the child's life – meal times, sleeping, bath-time, potty training, everything. For instance, if the bath is always run at 6 p.m. that is part of a child's life and their day's routine and they happily go along with it. There are no problems. If children always have their lunch at midday, then they automatically come and have their lunch. If you chop and change routines a lot, they will, of course, get used to it, but it may be at a cost, your unpredictability making it harder for them to cope. It is much better if the first few years of a child's life are orderly and peaceful. Routine means that the child knows what to expect so he doesn't have to constantly be told 'Come on, lunch now. Stop playing with that' – they know it's lunch. It's always been lunch.

So, the second Golden Rule is:
✦ Children need routine (not rewards).

Make an early start

Everything a child does has to be introduced sooner or later and then more or less stuck to. A routine introduced earlier is much more acceptable for a child than one imposed later on.

The difficulty often for parents is that they can't see into the future and so cannot appreciate which routines for their children they are going to find useful and which they are going to regret ever having started. I know many a parent who, after feeding the baby at 6 a.m. then took him into bed and played with him. The parents set up a routine which they enjoyed and so did the baby. But when the novelty had died away and they wanted to put him back into his bed instead of bringing him into theirs, he was so used to going in their bed that he was very, very angry when he could no longer join them.

But how can a new parent know how quickly babies absorb routine? It is only when you have a lot of experience with babies that you can predict what will be the likely outcome and which routines it is useful to establish and which ones to avoid. I have always thought that the routine of introducing a pot simply to get the child used to it, is one to establish early. But even if it is started later as long as it is introduced as a routine (see Chapter Five) rather than something that's going to happen from time to time, it will be accepted.

Starting routines later

If you start a routine later your child is able, quite rightly, to query what he is being encouraged to accept. This may be all right for some children, but it is potentially asking for problems. If you have delayed potty training your child will have lived a few more years and so instead of the pot already being part of his life, part of his routine, he can, and may, think 'I don't want to sit on the pot, I want to play.'

The idea of building in a routine may well smack of brain-washing, but because it is done in a gentle, lighthearted way it really is kinder to the child. In a way all habit learning is brain-washing. Some brain-washing is detestable, but the brain-washing you do in child-care is both for the child's benefit and your own by helping the child to fit into an adult world. Done early it does not worry a child and is a great help to the mother or other person in charge.

Don't go back to nappies

So, like with all 'brain-washing', once you have decided to build the pot into your child's life, you must be consistent and try and keep his routine the same. Don't stop and start potty training – keep going. So if you have started potty training and had a certain success and the child would appear to regress, don't scold but still put him on the pot just the same. Don't think 'I'll stop training him now and start again later', just keep on using the pot. Don't put a child back into nappies once you have taken him out of them, whether it has been a few weeks or even a few days, unless he becomes absolutely hysterical.

I once spoke to a rather worried mother who had first introduced the potty to her daughter when the daughter was two. As her daughter 'showed no interest' she didn't persevere and just tried 'on and off', with the result that her daughter, now three, was still using a nappy.

I told the mother that whenever she

introduced the pot to the child, whether the child showed interest or not, she must continue with her routine and not just try again periodically whenever the mood took her. With a routine it didn't take long before the little girl was happily using the pot, but if her mother had started with a consistent approach she could have been out of nappies a year earlier.

Of course, if at any stage your child takes a violent dislike to the pot, then I would put it away for a few weeks and then try again, but if the pot is very comfortable, your attitude is calm and you don't over-pot your child (put him on the pot too often or talk about the pot too much), this shouldn't happen. If there are other people who sometimes care for your child, then you must let them know your routine so the child is not confused in any way.

Children don't need rewards

Although I believe in encouraging a child in everything he does, I don't believe in rewards or bribes. For instance, one routine I would never use to get him to do what I want is the routine of star charts. I really do find it a most extraordinary thing to do. A bright child surely would say 'I don't want a star' – so what's the point of a star? Why should children eat their lunch or sit on their pot to please their parents? Why should the parents be pleased to have made their child eat the lunch? It's almost as if the parent needs the star chart to show how wonderful their cooking was or how persuasive they were to get their child on the pot.

I was never rewarded as a child and I have never

rewarded children. At my school if you were top of the class that was a reward enough in itself. And if you weren't top of the class it meant you couldn't be top of the class but that didn't mean you didn't do as well as you could have done. So really everyone should have been given a reward and instead no one was.

So many people, in any case, use rewards too early. I have observed a parent trying to bribe a child with a doll but the child was too young. She didn't understand that she would only be given the doll if she ate her lunch. She didn't realise that the doll was a reward which she was now not going to be given. The child desperately wanted the doll, but couldn't work out the connection between the food and the doll and was very upset.

*D*espairing mothers have told me about how they have tried to encourage their child to use a pot. They have tried everything they say – rewards, star charts, being cross, kind words, reading books, counting to 30 (before the nappy can be put on) and buying interesting shaped pots.

But all this is doing is entertaining the parent – it's not starting a routine, it's nothing to do with encouraging a child to use his pot. Children need the same thing every day as far as possible and they need a very calm casual approach. A routine should happen automatically. You should be neither cross nor ecstatic – using a pot or, later, the lavatory is part of the day and should be built-in to the routine of the day. If you try many different things with children and keep changing your approach, it is very confusing for the child.

In potty training, in particular, there should be no question of rewarding a child, after all, the point of the exercise is to encourage a child to use a pot primarily for his own comfort and well-being. Potty training is something you want to establish and when the child is able to be happy about sitting on a pot or a lavatory it is very satisfactory for all concerned.

✦ Remember: Children need routine
   (not rewards).

Silence Is Golden

Whatever the situation in a child's life you are coping with you must be fairly casual about anything you want the child to do or not do. If you make too much of it you may well achieve the opposite of what you want.

For this reason I would strongly advise against discussing pots or lavatories or anything to do with potty training with your child at any great length. If you introduce a pot to your child at nine months there is no need to talk about anything as the child is still young enough to accept what happens. But even if your child is older, eventually he is going to use a pot and then a lavatory like everybody else, and the aim is to introduce him to sitting on a pot in a casual way and talking about something a lot is not very casual.

Keep your thoughts to yourself
You would never say, 'We're going to get your hair cut tomorrow, we'll set off early so we can go to the green-

grocer first. No, we better not do that or we might be late for the hairdresser.' If you said all your thoughts out loud to a child as a stream of consciousness then your child would feel confused.

Children live in the present and the important thing with small children is that whatever happens should be *now* – whether it is sitting on a pot or getting your hair cut. If you tell a child that something is going to happen tomorrow afternoon it doesn't have any impact – it doesn't mean anything and he may keep on asking 'Are we going to do it now? Why isn't it now?' and then this irritates people enormously and I've heard people say 'I wish I'd never mentioned it.'

Don't prattle about the pot

No matter at what age you potty train a child it doesn't need to become a topic of conversation. Talking about anything with children too much is not a good idea. One shouldn't go on at great length about anything as if it was of great importance. It isn't. Potty training is just what happens and the more casually you treat it, the quicker it will happen as you would like it to. You never need to keep saying to a child 'Would you like a wee?' every few minutes. It must drive them mad the way adults ask them all the time.

Children can sense atmospheres just as adults can. They can feel it when adults are particularly nervous about getting something right and are expressing their nervousness through chat. The adults may think their casual banter is disguising their worries, but it is just making the child feel insecure.

*O*ne mother had given up potty training her son when he was two and a half and put him back into nappies. Six months later she was thrilled when her son used the pot (with very little prompting) both for urinating and once for defecating. She contacted me because out of the blue he insisted on having his nappy back on again. His bladder was so full that he began to leak and so she had given in and couldn't see that the situation would ever end.

I suggested that Mum was probably over-enthusiastic when he did use his pot and instead of just saying 'Well done' very casually and carrying on with life she was enthusiastic to the point of being irritating and provoking the boy to rebel. She was drawing attention to his using the pot instead of accepting it. It was being talked about too much. I said that she should put the pot away and then try again in a few weeks (behaving as if he'd been sitting on a pot all his life) and the next time he rebelled she shouldn't put the nappy back on. If his bladder should leak it would be a good thing and she would have to put up with wet and soiled pants for a few days. After that he should sit on the pot again.

A few words, gentle actions, a feeling that this is what happens every day, makes a child feel secure. Continually discussing a problem blows it out of all proportion and defeats its own ends.

The third Golden Rule is:

✦ Children don't want to talk about potty training (and you shouldn't either).

The less chat the better

Children today are so often treated as if they were little adults. I have had parents saying to me that when they ask a child why he or she doesn't like the loo the reply is 'Loos are horrible' or 'I like my nappy' or whatever. The point is not to ask the child, not to talk about things so much. At such an early age in a child's development it really doesn't seem fair to ask them to make a decision or to have to rationalise what they are thinking. You should be in control and making their decisions for them. That spells security. Everything should be all right as far as they are concerned without them even thinking about it. The age to start talking to a child and deferring a little more to him is not before eight years. Trying to talk to a two- or three-year-old as if they were much older is not fair.

Don't ask them to choose

The reason parents often assume their two-year-olds have views on everything is because they do say 'I don't want to wear that shirt'. They may well be saying this not because they really don't like the shirt, but because the last time they wore those trousers they had a different shirt on and they want the same shirt again with those trousers. That to them spells security. Of course, it may be that the shirt itches or it is too tight, but I think a parent may well interpret their two-year-old child's dislike of the shirt as an adult dislike of a shirt and presume therefore that their child has views on most subjects. I think this may be why many adults ask their children to choose things or to explain their views. Children of this age shouldn't be expected to choose and have opinions – it gives them an insecure feeling.

When decisions are made for them, those decisions are, in a way, barriers and within them they feel safe.

I have often overheard people saying to children things like 'You're not a baby, you're a big girl now'. One little girl I was asked to help was only twenty-seven months old and her mother thought that she didn't want to wear her nappy because she didn't want to grow up. But a child of this age cannot conceive of what being 'grown-up' means – after all 'grown-up', in the sense of being an adult, is nothing to do with behaviour, it is when you have lived a number of years. What this child saw was that 'being grown-up' meant she would no longer wear nappies. It had been offered as an alternative to wearing nappies 'Come on, you're not a baby anymore, you're a big girl. You're grown-up now, you don't need to wear a nappy'.

This story shows that the less you say to a child the better. The mother had wanted to put a concept into the child's head in order to make the child feel happy, superior even (as though being grown-up is in itself superior). It had backfired and the child was using the mother's concept against her. It was a wonderful excuse not to wear her nappy. She could just say 'I don't want to be grown-up'.

Aids that don't help
There are quite a few children's books and videos in the shops aimed at helping the small child to become potty trained. I am very much against these instructional aids for the same reason I am against talking to children about

potty training. It seems a terrible waste of money to buy a book or a video showing children how to sit on a pot. It's unnecessary. They also won't want to read or watch it everyday on the pot. They'll get used to it like they get used to all story books and it won't have any impact any more. Whereas adults are used to following instructions from a book or video, toddlers aren't. When Humpty Dumpty falls off a wall, they don't think 'Humpty's fallen off a wall so I will too'. It has no significance for them. So if you buy them a book or a video in which a child is on a pot it doesn't mean anything. You might think it's a fun thing to do and for two or three days they will look at it, but they won't copy the child in the picture because they are too young to make the connection.

Teddy goes to the pot

Aim, as always, to keep a relaxed approach to potty training. I have sometimes placed a little doll's pot on which teddy or a favourite doll has perched next to the child because just as teddy shares the lunch and goes to bed, teddy can sit on the pot as well. I did have a child who often wriggled about on the pot not really wanting to go and I would say 'Hang on a minute and teddy will sit on the pot too'. The fact that teddy wasn't going to do anything was never commented on, because the child would use the pot or would not use the pot according to how he was feeling, but teddy was sitting on the pot too. The whole point is to keep it a casual part of the day. If teddy is a very close part of the child's life he can join in, but he isn't a 'must'.

Be on your child's side

If the child rebels against the pot I would put it right away in a cupboard and then a couple of weeks later I would try again. In those two weeks I wouldn't mention the pot once. And it is vital that you say to adults 'Please don't talk about it. We are going to try again later'. But if someone inadvertently says 'Doesn't Mark sit on his potty any more?' show that you are on the child's side. Say firmly, 'No, he didn't find it comfortable. He didn't like it very much. He's going to try again a bit later on.'

If you are going to talk about your child in front of him – always be on his side. Never put him down. After all, if *you* don't stick up for him, who's going to? People don't realise that what they say in front of children has such an influence. If you tell them that they're wonderful it gives them a feeling of safety and if you put them down it has the reverse effect.

Older children sometimes make a jokey remark if their younger brother or sister does wet the bed or their pants. 'Look Mummy, Mary's done a wee all over the floor – ugh!' Be quite calm, don't get annoyed with the one who's weed or with the siblings. Just say 'So did you when you were two' and mop it up. Don't talk about accidents, wet beds, soiled pants or anything. It's a nuisance to you, because you're busy and the last thing you need is to clean it up, but it is so important for the child to know that you don't really mind.

Keep mum at the doctor's

Again with older children, if you want to take a child of four to the doctor about bladder or bowel control then don't talk about it in front of the child. Hand the doctor a very clearly written letter which very briefly explains what you are worried about, so that you don't have to mention it too much in front of the child. Once a child is over five you will have to explain to him why he is being taken. Of course, you will know not to worry him. Just explain simply 'It's such a nuisance for you that you sometimes do it in your pants so we thought we would ask the doctor if there was a reason that you can't wait.' Take them into your confidence, don't make a big fuss about it.

◆Remember: Children don't want to talk about potty training (and you shouldn't either).

Look Through Your Child's Eyes

All children are individuals and most children will oppose the person that is trying to make them do various things. If you try and force your child or put pressure on him in any way he will fight against you, so you must always seem to be fairly relaxed. Your child is a little person and must be treated as a person in his own right – with respect.

The fourth Golden Rule is:

◆Every child is an individual whose rights and feelings should be respected.

With potty training if a child is put on the pot obsessively at the beginning, that is, 'over-potted' then the child will probably be adamant he is never going to sit on that pot again, so potty training must be started gradually and casually. Every day a child is growing more and more into a person and accepts less and less. An older child may well see the pot as an intrusion into his life – try and see it through his eyes. You get much better results if you don't fuss about it – if you think to yourself as you sit your child on the pot 'It really doesn't matter whether he uses it or not, but he'll enjoy it.' Force is counter productive. Keep it light-hearted, don't be intense about it. Never, ever force a child to sit on a potty. If you are aggressive about it the child becomes fearful of the pot and it takes much, much longer and causes a lot of unhappiness. It's another reason for starting early because that way you know you'll have years ahead in which your child can learn what the potty is for. If you start later you may have family pressures – or outside ones – that will mean you are worried about how long potty training is going to take; the child can feel these worries.

One mother contacted me at her wits' end. She had just moved into rented accommodation and was planning to move again once she had found something suitable to buy. She had a son who was almost three and an eight-month-old daughter of whom the son was clearly jealous. A month before they had moved house the first time he had started soiling his pants and the problem was getting worse. The trouble was that the whole atmosphere was charged with worry and the little boy was very mixed up and muddled. Of course, his potty training problems were adding to his mother's worry.

I told her that although he might continue soiling his pants until the atmosphere had settled down it might also just stop as suddenly as it started. She must avoid mentioning the problem to anyone and try and be his friend by just casually suggesting that she'd put the pot in the corner and he could take it when he needed it. If he didn't use it she must just clean him up and with as little fuss as possible.

Children need to feel secure

Little children are really rather like dogs. They can feel atmosphere. They really don't quite know what is going on but they can feel a happy atmosphere and they can feel a disturbing, worrying atmosphere. Of course they are part of the household and you can't say 'I mustn't worry about so and so' because you can't stop worrying, but as far as the child is concerned, you must be reassuring and *try* to make his day just the same as it always was. Little children find comfort in a familiar routine. Being asked to choose or make decisions is stressful for children, and they shouldn't have to do it. It makes for a sense of security if you do the deciding and the child doesn't have to think.

Changes can hinder training

As with everything in your child's life, potty training is affected by atmosphere and you must make allowances for this. If there is a lot going on (moving house, holidays, new baby, different helpers in the house) or something exciting is happening or the child is absorbed in his play, then he may well not use the pot. If it is something exciting then a young child does not want to waste time sitting on the pot and if there is a lot of turmoil that they don't understand then they may well be feeling tense and insecure. They can't shut out their worries and think about perching on a pot, so they just do whatever they have to do in their pants. An aggressive approach also affects the atmosphere – it sets potty training back as the child won't want to relax enough to sit on the pot.

Potty training is not only affected by a specific feeling of insecurity in the child's life, such as a parent going away, but it can also be affected by the family's attitude towards him.

I met a woman once who spoke to me about her five-year-old boy who she complained was very unco-operative in every way. There was a wall between the two of them. She was continually giving him orders and he reciprocated by taking food when she wasn't looking and weeing on the floor. It was an extreme case, but one in which the child was using his urine to state how unhappy he was with the way she was treating him. I suggested she must change her whole attitude and stop giving him orders of any kind and start respecting him as a human being.

If the atmosphere in the house is not sympathetic to the child and he is punished, even if not very severely, frustrated and put down for doing, or not doing, certain things it will cause problems in every sphere – food, sleeping, relationships and potty training. A child being forced to eat is an extreme example of a worrying scenario, as is that of a child who is always being put down: 'Don't be so silly' or 'Don't throw that' – after all, throwing is part of a child's development. You may even find that a tense child has a few more 'accidents' than a relaxed child as children who are worried about a situation go to the loo a lot to urinate and he may not always be able to get there in time. So have a friendly approach to your child so that whatever happens is fine.

Children take in more than you think

Perhaps because adults don't always realise how much quite small children take in, they unthinkingly make hurtful comparisons. With everything to do with children, people do compare. I so often hear children being compared to each other – when they go to sleep, when they feed themselves, when they go to the pot and so on, and so on – even brother against brother – in the child's presence and it is not a good thing to do. It is very damaging for the child to hear himself being compared unfavourably with another child and so unfair, as you don't usually compare adults – or at least if you do, you do it behind their backs. Every child is an individual with his own abilities and some can do some things and some others; to hear how slow or stupid he is compared to so-and-so does sap his confidence.

There are generalisations that can be made about the sexes. For example, it's more or less a general rule that girls are potty trained earlier than boys, so it's certainly not fair to compare the sexes or expect your son to be as quick as your daughter was. Please don't say 'He's so slow' about your son, if you had a daughter first. He's being as fast as he can.

Apart from making comparisons grown-ups often talk about their children with their friends when the children are present, thinking the children don't hear what they are saying. It may not affect the child to hear himself being discussed as in, for instance, 'Johnny and I went to the zoo yesterday. We had such fun, Johnny did like the tigers' – positive things like that don't do any harm.

Children have rights, too

But although it's harmless, I wouldn't speak about a child to other people when the child was present. If you think about it it is almost an insult, because you don't do it about adults. You would never say 'We went to the theatre and my husband thought it was wonderful.' You would always add 'Didn't you, darling?' You would never talk about him as if he wasn't there. You can involve the child too: 'We went to Granny's yesterday – you did enjoy her cherry cake, didn't you Johnny?'

If it is something you want to discuss about him such as potty training or eating problems or anything 'negative', then wait until you are alone with your friend. It is unfair to discuss your problems with your child in front of him as though he can't hear what you are saying. I have observed children being able to understand simple things from the age of one and a quarter. You can see by the expression on their faces that they know exactly what you are saying .

♦ Remember: Every child is an individual whose rights and feelings should be respected.

CHAPTER THREE

Basic Training Equipment

Y OU NEED VERY LITTLE EQUIPMENT FOR POTTY training and could make do without any, but I have seen little children perching and balancing on a loo and think that having a pot and later a little seat to sit on is probably quite nice and much more convenient. Of course, from the parent's point of view, they are yet more things that add to the clutter of child care.

Choosing the pot

It is important to buy a comfortable pot so that your child is happy to sit on it. We always used to have enamel pots which inevitably got chipped and were cold for little bums. Plastic pots are always warm and comfortable; I would choose a straight-sided one so that it can't tip over. The type intended for a boy, with a little shield in front, can also be used by a girl so you might as well choose this one if you have a girl and then it will do if you ever need one, such as for visiting boy children. You can now buy pots in all different shapes and sizes and if Granny wants to buy one looking like a tractor then why not, but I would suggest just buying a simple pot. It doesn't clutter up your home as much and is easy to take on outings. A larger pot is great fun but unnecessary.

Care and cleaning

When I empty the pot after it has been used I always add some water to the contents to help tip it out into the loo and then add a little more water and tip that out too. If any faeces are left on the pot I would wipe it round with loo paper and then add a few drops of disinfectant and wipe it round again and rinse with water. Never leave any bleach in a pot because the ammonia in the child's urine combined with the bleach can produce toxic fumes.

Lavatory seat and stool

Once a child is three you can start introducing the idea that he can sit on the lavatory, but you will need to get a small seat to fit on top of the existing seat so the child can sit comfortably. If you haven't got one already I would also buy a box or a small stool for him to put his feet on when sitting on the loo. Some of the boxes that are sold for this purpose are not high enough for it to be possible for the child to rest his feet on.

I always lift a small child on to the child's seat. They can scramble on but sometimes the little seat slides about when they get on, so I lift them up and put them firmly on the seat with their feet resting on the stool. I always wash the child's seat once a week and make sure I don't leave it on the loo. It is so easy for you to have a routine of removing it and propping it up behind the lavatory. Although, as I said earlier a small loo seat isn't essential, I have watched children clinging precariously on to each side of the adults' loo seat and I think it must be so uncomfortable for them.

I was once contacted by a grandfather whose grandson, aged four and a half, came to stay with him every day whilst his mother was at work. He was worried because this little boy would only go to the loo after a telephone call from his mother asking him to do so. I said that the grandfather should stop worrying and give up asking his grandson if he needed to go to the loo – he would notice if the little boy did, as he would wriggle about and if he did do it in his pants then that wasn't the end of the world.

I also mentioned that many small people would much rather use the pot or the lavatory in their own home with their own mother and never use lavatories or pots in a strange house or school, so it might be a good idea if the boy's mother bought one of those little loo seats (and a footstool too if she could afford it) to fit on the grandfather's lavatory. She should say to her son 'I bought this so that when you are at grandpa's house you can fit it on his lavatory and it will be your special seat.' I explained that because the lavatory seat has been given to him by his mother he will associate it with her and it will bridge the gap between his two lives. I told the grandfather not to mention the loo seat but to leave it to the boy to make the first move.

Disposable nappies and training pants

I found towelling nappies so much easier than disposable ones when potty-training a child as they would just pull down. They would have loosened a little during the time the child had been wearing them and dropped down easily, whether fastened with one safety pin or two. Of course, afterwards, the nappy (the old one if it was dry or a new one) had to be pinned on again properly, but taking it off was easy. A disposable nappy might be quicker to put back on if you haven't had practice with the towelling type, but it is more difficult to take off and on the whole cannot be re-used even if it is clean unless it is pinned on.

So many things are offered to parents that are not necessities (although they may well be a boon to working mothers). Disposable nappies and training pants are items that are expensive and non-essential. Furthermore neither is environmentally friendly and although they may help you dispose of your child's offerings, they contribute to the disposal problem of the planet. It seems to me that whenever a product is preceded by the word 'training' (such as pants, beaker, spoon, etc.) it is a product invented by the manufacturer solely to make money and that all it does for the child is give him another unnecessary skill to learn.

Mattress cover

I always used a waterproof cover on a child's mattress. In the old days we had a rubber mackintosh mattress cover and I would put a glove sheet over it and then a flannelette sheet on top of that as the glove sheet was very thin and sleeping on a waterproof cover can make you so hot. These days most mattresses are sold in a waterproof cover, but if yours isn't, you should keep it covered especially when you leave a child's nappy off at night from the age of three. If yours is, then I would cover it with a towel and then put a glove sheet on top of that, otherwise it can be very hot and unpleasant for the child.

Books and videos

You don't need to buy your child books or videos about potty training as I have explained on page 34, but you might want to buy them a new book in a series they like to look at especially for when they are on their pot.

CHAPTER FOUR

The Easy Way

M Y MANY YEARS' EXPERIENCE AS A NANNY HAVE convinced me that the way of potty training that is described in this chapter has more advantages and fewer problems than any other.

Nine months

Once a nine-month-old baby has finished breakfast, I sit him on his pot. I place him with his back to the play-pen and using a square muslin nappy tie him firmly but loosely to the bars so that he can't fall over onto his nose. You may be horrified at the idea of tying your baby in this way, but it is really no different to support-ing him with your arm. The folded muslin goes round the tummy, but higher (under the ribs) rather than lower, or it would make the child feel sick. I don't tie it tightly, just tight enough to hold the baby firmly upright because if he is not firmly tied the child leans forward. He can't fall off the pot but he is nicely and firmly supported. Some babies at this age can sit up firmly without help, but most babies are wobbly, so this makes a safe and comfortable position for them.

Pot bound

I don't say anything when I'm putting him on the pot. I give him a teddy or a little book, and I leave him for ten minutes while I'm getting on with my usual tasks. I'm always nearby, never out of earshot, but it isn't absolutely necessary to stay in the room. If, when I take the baby off ten minutes later, he had done something I might say 'Oh, look what you've done, clever boy', but in a calm way, but if the pot is empty, I certainly don't scold the child.

If a baby boy has urinated you don't need to do anything, for a baby girl I would mop with a tissue. If the child has defecated I always clean up with a piece of damp cotton wool and then dry thoroughly with a muslin nappy. I then put on new cream and a new nappy (if the old one was wet or soiled). I wouldn't use the pot again that day but carry on with nappies as usual.

Using a chair pot

If your baby can sit up well then you could use a chair pot which would hold him in with a wooden bar, but as it is a new situation I think he would squirm around and might try and stand up so I prefer to use a muslin nappy. I only tie a baby to the playpen (or any other piece of heavy furniture) until he can sit quite firmly without falling off, which is some time between a year and eighteen months. Then I put the pot in the corner of the room so that he can't fall off backwards. But I tie the child on for quite a few months as you don't want him to get bored and walk off the pot. By this later stage you could certainly use a chair pot.

The best time to pot

After breakfast is a very good time to put a baby on a pot. Children almost always empty their bowels at that time (and you have one less soiled nappy to deal with) and it also enables you to clear the breakfast table at the same time. But if you have other children and breakfast is too chaotic you could wait until you have come home from the school run to put your baby on the pot. He may already have defecated, but you will still be introducing the pot into his day.

Pot on the spot

In the old days we usually had linoleum on the nursery floor; the bathroom was usually close by so any spillage or soilage could easily be cleaned up. Today it can be quite unhygienic with children playing in the kitchens or carpeted rooms. When you start potty training it's not easy to move a child from one room to another. He just has to use the pot wherever he is. Once he has bladder control you can keep the pot in the bathroom and he should go to it there.

Ten months

Once the baby has been using the pot every day after breakfast for a month, if you are not able to keep up the routine (because the baby is ill or you are away or some other reason) don't worry. Simply start again when you can, putting the baby on twice a day – after tea as well. Leave him with a toy or a book for ten minutes or so. Don't get involved in a long telephone call to your friend and leave the baby on for much longer or he will get bored and begin to resent the pot.

Eleven months

Now I would start putting the baby on the pot after lunch as well. He should still be perfectly happy about going on the pot. If for any reason he is not then I would stop doing it for a short space of time – a couple of weeks. Just put the pot out of sight and don't talk about it to anyone in the child's presence or to the child himself. He will still be wearing nappies all day and night but will by now be sitting on the pot three times a day. You should have very few soiled nappies; all his stools should be going in the pot.

One year

At one year the child is going on the pot three times a day and should still be perfectly happy about it. If everything is going well then I would start putting him on the pot a fourth time, after coming back from an outing – whether to the park or to the shops or to visit a friend – so long as he remains happy. It doesn't matter whether he uses the pot or not. You are getting him used to a fixed routine (the three times a day visits) and also to a spontaneous routine (depending on what time your outing is). When you put him on the pot after the outing, again leave him for up to ten minutes, but no longer.

Why not start potting at one?

I am often asked why I don't start putting children on a pot at a year because nine months seems so young. But by now your child is a year and you will notice that he is able to achieve more things. He can sit up alone and can very often crawl, he can use a spoon unaided – one might say he is restless, ambitious almost. Introducing a pot now would be an irritant when he wants to scrabble about. It is a frustration to him, he cannot do the adventurous things he is beginning to enjoy. If you start at nine months sitting on a comfortable pot is like sitting on a comfortable chair, he is not going to resent it and if you don't overdo it, it becomes an acceptable part of his daily routine.

Eighteen months

By eighteen months your child is sitting on the pot four times a day. By this age he may well be fetching the pot for himself when you come back from an outing or after the meal. Even if they haven't yet got bladder or bowel control by now children know that the little plastic container you've got sitting in the bathroom is part of their day.

Instead of saying 'Don't play with that – it's not a toy', you can quickly peel down their pants and sit them on it. You must still secure them somehow, otherwise after a few seconds of sitting down they get up again and run around. You can divert their attention by giving them a little book but I would still fasten them to the pot with the muslin nappy or give them a chair pot – as long as they couldn't get out of it. If you have fastened them in every time they have been on the pot they won't resent it.

Don't overdo it

I wouldn't put them on the pot many more than four times a day or they begin to resent it. If they are dry after their nap then I would put them on the pot (just saying 'Why not do it in the pot?' very casually) or at another time of day when you know your child is ready to go. However, certainly don't pot them more than five times a day.

At eighteen months children can recognise the fact that when they sit on the pot they do defecate – that is what it is for. A child of this age can usually tell you after he has defecated, but not before, so don't ever, ever scold or punish him if he does defecate in his nappy just after you have taken him off the pot. It is irritating but understandable because he doesn't yet know that he should *only* do it in the pot and may not yet have the control. I have known children at this stage who one felt had complete bladder and bowel control but had several relapses. I have also known children who at this stage had no bladder or bowel control at all.

Twenty months to two years

At this stage you sometimes get an idea that the child is very soon going to be able to give up nappies. This is because each time you change him you find the nappy is still dry and you put him on the pot and he uses it. Also, very often a child is beginning to get the idea that that is why he is sitting on the pot and I have known children sit down on the pot fully dressed – and nappy on. They are trying to tell you they are ready to have their nappies removed.

'Nappy off' time

Very often at this age a child resents having his nappy on because it is such a bore having to lie down as the nappy is either pinned or stuck on. It is so frustrating and he will say 'No nappy' or 'Nappy off' or something. Not because he thinks it is beneath his dignity but because it is such a nuisance. That is your moment not to put it on any longer, except at nap times, for long outings and at night.

By this age most children are acquiring bowel control. A child will begin to look a little uncomfortable and hold onto his bottom which means that he is ready to be put onto the pot. Wet pants still occur on and off – don't make a fuss about this at all. When the child now urinates he empties his bladder, it's not just a trickle, and so a certain length of time does go by between wees.

How to tell when they need the pot?
You can tell when a child needs the pot as he will squirm a little bit or grab his crotch or maybe go quiet for a minute, concentrating. Even if children are in the middle of wetting their pants I would quickly put them on the pot. I wouldn't be cross, but I would certainly try to catch what's left.

At this stage although they will start to get bladder control, they won't yet be able to 'hang on' until they get to the pot. That will come within the next six months to a year. If a child is in his highchair in the middle of the meal and I can tell he needs to defecate then I would ideally leave him to dirty his pants and enjoy the rest of his meal (he won't mind dirty pants and it is less disruptive for him), but if you are in a family situation it can be very smelly. I would remove him quickly and calmly as it is so much easier to clean up a child if you have caught him half way through, but I wouldn't be cross or even talk about it.

From nappy to pants
The next stage of the routine is for children to wear

pants instead of a nappy. It is so much easier to take pants down than unfasten nappies and very, very soon the child accept the pants and doesn't really miss the nappies. When the nappy is no longer there on the bottom for them to urinate into, they sometimes still wet their pants, but I don't see the point of letting them run around without pants to save the washing. The child would get cold and you'd have to clean up the floor anyway. In the garden or on the beach I would always take their clothes off if the sun wasn't too hot, but it isn't a necessary part of potty training. Why have children if you mind washing their pants?

Before children are what is known as 'reliable' I would always keep the pot in the corner behind a chair because I would want to keep it handy. If you have to run to the bathroom to get it it would be too late. The moment I see a small girl wanting to do a urinate or defecate I would quickly pull her pants down and sit her on the pot. If it was a little boy, he could either sit down to pee or (if he has had experience of standing and weeing into a pot) I would hold the pot underneath the winkie and guide the stream into the pot. They certainly don't need to be tied on to the pot anymore at this stage because they will know what the pot is for.

Flushed with pride
By the time they were two my children always knew what the pot was for and they all had bowel and bladder control – although that does not mean that they did not have a few 'accidents'. Children do get very excited once they understand the purpose of the pot. They have great pride in what they have done. They pick the pot up and carry it to show you whatever is in there.

Until the child is two and a half I always put a nappy on whenever he is asleep, at night or during a nap, and if we are going out for longer than an hour.

A mother of a little girl, not yet two, once told me that her daughter had refused to let her put a nappy on her from the age of nineteen months. Although she was dry during the day she was now having a tantrum every night, and every nap time, because she did not want to wear her nappy then either. Her mother was worried because she didn't want to have to change a wet bed every night. I said that she should do what her daughter wanted. She did and her daughter was dry both in the night and at nap times.

Two and a half years

By this stage children have enough control to be able to get to the bathroom in time, so the pot can be put there. Emptying their own pot amuses children because it is like playing with water, tipping the water in to rinse it. They have seen you emptying the pot into the loo and so they want to do it too. If a young child wants to do it and starts picking up the pot I would lend a hand and then I would say 'I'll just put a drop of water in' and then I would do that and rinse it round and then we'd pour that in together.

If they had defecated I used to wipe their botty with a soft tissue or cotton wool and then drop a muslin nappy over the pot to stop it smelling whilst I pulled their pants up and tucked their vest in. They would then run back into the nursery, having forgotten about it. This stopped the 'problem' of the child wanting to help tip their motion into the loo, but if they want to help then let them – with your supervision.

Portable pots

At this age I no longer put a child's nappy on when we are going out. I put them on the pot as usual before setting out and I always take their pot, some loo paper, baby wipes, a spare pair of underpants and any creams and lotions that are needed. Often children won't go on a strange loo (see page 45) so taking the pot is essential. They used to make special PVC bags with a box compartment at the bottom with a zip round it in which to transport the pot, and in the top you could keep other things for the child.

Peeing in the park

Children vary in how often they need to urinate. If a litte boy needs to do a pee in the park he can go behind a tree and spend a penny. A little girl finds crouching down a problem – they tend to do it over their shoes and underpants – so nannies would lift them up, remove their underpants and hold them between their knee and their buttocks, spread their legs a little bit and with their back towards you so that the wee would go on to the grass. Lots of nannies wouldn't allow their children to do it in the park – it was considered rude – and so children quite often wet their pants. I thought this was so unkind especially as little boys need to go more often than girls and it was so easy to poke their winkies out of the side of the leg of the very short shorts they used to wear. Some people would sit their children on the pot in the park.

Three years

Some children are still much happier sitting on a pot when they are three but lots of children are able to sit on a loo with a child's seat and a box for their feet. I never, ever insist on a child giving up the pot because quite often children have a fear of the lavatory – there's a long space between their bottom and the U-bend and children are very often afraid of that. An adult saying 'Well, you're big now – you should use the loo' is just the sort of thing that might make a nervous child more nervous still.

Bag a loo seat

You can now get such adequate child seats that using the loo may not worry children. I just introduce it casually: 'I've got this new seat and stool. You can sit here instead of sitting on the pot.' They might be very pleased but if they don't want to use it then don't make them. I've never had a child who didn't want to sit on the loo seat. If smaller children are interested in the loo and want to try it because they have seen their siblings or parents using it, then why not, as long as you hold them because they might lean forward and fall off.

When a child of three goes to the loo I remove his pants completely as it is awkward when they slip down to the ankles or sometimes even drop off anyway. I always lift my child on to the loo seat although if a busy child removes the pants by himself and clambers up the step onto the loo I certainly wouldn't stop him. After a child has urinated I would mop him and after he has defecated I just clean him and then wash my hands and put his pants back on.

Some children want to wipe their bottoms

themselves. Allow them to but always supervise them as they can't at this age make a good job of it. I would say 'Well done. I'll just have a look and see if you've made it nice and clean', then pull up their pants (or let them do it if they wanted to) and finally wash their hands.

Patience pays off

It does drive you mad if you have the sort of children who want to do everything themselves. I see parents hurrying their children along and saying 'You're old enough to do it yourself', but waiting for children to put their own pants on can take so much longer than just pulling them up yourself. Children do love to do it and very soon they are expert at it. It is frustrating for an adult but you must be patient as in no time at all they will be adept at doing it.

Boys standing up to wee

By the time little boys are three they would be standing up by the loo to urinate. Usually they can stand on the floor to do it but sometimes I have to lift them up off the ground, holding them under their arms to help them aim straight, if their legs were not quite long enough. Using a little stool is a bit dicey because they can fall off it. When a boy first starts I lift the seat up and pull his trousers down to the ankles and show him how to put his winkie over the loo. Afterwards I say 'Shake the drip off' and show him how to shake his winkie. I then pull his pants back up – unless he wants to – and lastly rinse his hands under the tap.

Nappy off when sleeping

By the time children are three they can dispense with a nappy at night-time. It will on the whole have been dry so there is no point in leaving it on, but I would remove it at three anyway. I do this because some children automatically wet into a nappy as they feel unconsciously that it is there to wet, but if you remove it for one or two nights they will wet their beds but then after that they won't. Sensing that the nappy is no longer on, the child might wake to go to the pot or to the loo or they might not wake.

With some children it does take longer than a couple of nights but you should persevere and not discuss it with the child. I would just say to him on the first night 'We won't put on a nappy tonight. We'll put these little cotton pants on instead' and then leave it off and put a pair of underpants on under his pyjamas. If the child says 'I want my nappy on' then I would leave it on and try again in a couple of weeks with no discussion about the subject again.

Keep it casual

Don't say 'We'll leave it off because you're a big boy now', just be casual and leave it off and if they ask 'Where's my nappy tonight?' you can simply reply 'I just thought we'd leave it off.' I think they'll be quite intrigued. It must feel nice and free not having a nappy on although nannies did always put underpants on under the child's nightie. (At this age both girls and boys used to wear nighties.) Today it is more likely that both the boys and the girls will be wearing pyjamas. Do make a point of providing simple nightwear so it is easy for the child – all-in-one sleeping suits are almost impossible for a child in a hurry to cope with.

Once children no longer sleep in nappies I leave the potty in their room (near their bed) so that if they wake in the night or when they wake in the morning they can use the pot. I leave the sides of their cots down so they can get out. I don't leave any loo paper as children don't use it. Children rarely use the pot in the night but if they wake early in the morning they often nip out of bed and use it.

Potting the child at night

Some people believe in sitting children on a pot at 10 p.m., hoping that this will stop them wetting their beds. The children are usually fast asleep and as the pot is put in their bed they don't have to move, but it seems to me so unnecessary. The pot suggests that they should spend a penny and so they usually do.

Sometimes a child didn't urinate and I've known people to wait for ages. I never did this as it seemed to me that the parents were training their child to spend a penny at 10 p.m. every evening. Often the child was potted and still wet his bed. It may have helped some children but I think it's an unnecessary habit to start, rather unkind and often later regretted. To parents who change their minds and ask me how to stop it, I tell them to stop immediately, expect one or two wet beds and the problem will be over.

On the other hand, if a child wakes crying in the middle of the night, perhaps because of a bad dream, it is a good idea to ask them if they want to use the lavatory or the pot before tucking them back down again. It is like starting the night again and it is worth doing.

Drinking during the night
If a child wants a drink at night I would certainly not refuse him. It was thought that if a child had nothing to drink after 5 p.m. until the next morning he wouldn't wet his bed, but if a child is thirsty he must have something to drink. If he is a child who drinks at teatime and drinks at bedtime and drinks in the middle of the night then he will need to sit on the pot and get rid of it, which makes for a restless night. It shouldn't mean that the child wets his bed, but rather that he has to keep jumping out of bed. Some children do drink large amounts both during the day and at night. A child of three doesn't need two bottles of milk before bedtime. He doesn't really need anything before he goes to bed and unless you introduce a night-time drink he won't ask for it.

Four years

There is not a great deal of difference between a four- and a three-year-old child. He is possibly speaking more clearly and can tell you when he wants to go. He is gaining wider understanding so can grasp that if you were going on a long walk he will need to go before-hand. If he is a child who always wants to spend pennies then you should take him to the loo and just pop him on before an outing. He might say 'I don't want to go' in which case I would just say 'All right then, I just thought you might.' I would never say 'Do you want to go to the loo?' because there comes a point when children want to do the opposite and then, even if they do want to go to the loo, because you have suggested it, they will refuse to go.

I still make sure their bottoms are clean at this age,

and usually wipe them myself. My children often used to bend down on all fours like a dog so I could make a good job of it.

Five years

By the time children are five they can usually wipe their own bottoms but if they don't want to then I would always do it for them. Some children like to do it as it is copying what you have done to them. Initially I just tear off two or three pieces of loo paper to show them how much is needed. I would fold it over and hand it to them. Left to their own devices children enjoy playing with loo paper and if the amount they had taken looked a bit extravagant I would just say 'Please don't use so much' and take some of it away. Some children don't want to do it for themselves and you must respect their feelings. When they start doing it you must supervise as they can get sore if the wiping is inadequate.

I allow children to wipe their bottoms the way they want to, although it is much easier for a girl to wipe her bottom the 'wrong' way (from back to front). I wouldn't make a big fuss about it. In any case, if you have always done it correctly (from front to back) to the girl she will feel automatically which is the right way, and will copy the way you do it.

Washing their hands

Until children are five I usually wipe their bottoms. They see me wash my hands so they are learning how important it is and if they wipe their bottoms before they are five, then I would supervise them washing their hands too. I would put some water in a bowl and give them a small piece of soap. They usually enjoy it because they like playing with water.

At five boys may wear trousers with flies, although if wearing shorts with wide legs they can still pull the leg of the shorts over in order to urinate through the leg. With long trousers they have to use the flies or pull them down.

CHAPTER FIVE

Starting Later

I HAVE ALWAYS INTRODUCED A CHILD TO A POT AT NINE months, but if your child is older and you haven't yet done so there is no cause for worry. Tonight I suggest you read chapters Two (Four Golden Rules) and Four (The Easy Way) and then I would start tomorrow morning. But don't make a big fuss about it. Even though you are hoping that he will use the pot tomorrow morning, it's best to be realistic – he may not.

Don't let a new baby or new house or anything else new interfere with your potty training, just don't expect too much. Carry on with it – try *very* hard not to scold if there is a bit of a lapse and, as always, try to keep the child's life as settled as possible.

Under two years

If your child is under two years old then you must secure him to the pot (see page 48). Be very casual, just make sure that he is comfortable. You wouldn't have to secure your child if he was used to the pot, but as you are just introducing it he will find it rather strange so you must make sure it is a comfortable pot, and not too low. Put him on the pot for ten minutes after breakfast and give him a book to look at, or a favourite toy, and just stay pottering about in the room to keep him company.

Pot luck

If your child doesn't use the pot I would just remove him after ten minutes and put his nappy back on. You are simply introducing him to the feel of a pot. If he does use the pot just lift him off immediately after he's used it (no need to leave him sitting there any longer), mop him clean, and casually say 'Well done', but don't make a big fuss about it.

What if he refuses?

I suggest you continue to put him on the pot once a day for a couple of weeks and then start putting him on twice a day (after breakfast and after tea). After a couple more weeks I would put him on after lunch as well and then after a further two weeks I would put him on again after his daytime sleep or on return from an outing.

If he takes against the pot and refuses to use it, just hide it away for three weeks and don't refer to it at all in front of the child. I would then bring it out in the same relaxed way and try again.

Two years and over

If you are starting potty training when the child is older, just introduce the subject very calmly after breakfast one day. I would say 'I've got this nice, comfortable pot for you to sit on so that you can do your wees and poos in here instead of in your nappy and then we can put them down the loo. Why don't you sit on it and do a wee or a poo – whatever you need to do.'

I would then put him on it and say 'Isn't it comfy?' and then I would get his favourite book, or a new book that you know he'll like, and teddy, so he is relaxed and say 'Do have a look at the book for a few minutes whilst I clear the table and then I'll come and read it to you.' Or, if you think he won't stay there without you, then I would sit down next to him and read it to him straightaway. If he's very fond of teddy you could have bought teddy a new pot too – it all helps to keep the situation light-hearted.

Introduce him to the pot

A child over two probably will need to be sat with for ten minutes or he'll jolly well get up and run away. Talk about all sorts of things or read him a little book, because it will be very strange for him sitting on something he has never sat on (or perhaps even seen) before. Maybe when you put him on it you could say 'I thought you might like to do pee-pee in the pot just like I do when I go to the loo – or you might do a poo.' If after ten minutes he has done nothing take him off and put a clean nappy on him and try again the next morning. Carry on putting him on the pot once a day for two weeks and then put him on it twice a day.

If he does a wee or a poo then take him off straightaway. 'Well, look what you've done. Jolly good, clever old you. We can now tip it in the loo.' Then I would clean his bottom without talking about it and *not* put his nappy back on either. I would clean the pot and leave it out and after two or three hours if he was still dry then I would put him on it again and say 'We'll have lunch in a minute, let's see if you can do another pee-

pee in a pot' and again sit with him for ten minutes or less if he uses it.

Try and try again

If he doesn't use it I'd still keep his nappy off and risk an 'accident', unless we were going out, when I would put the nappy back on until we got home. He probably would have wet his nappy by now, but if it was dry I'd sit him on the pot and say 'Perhaps you can do another pee-pee like this morning.' I would then just keep the nappy off until bedtime. I would keep the pot available and take him every two or three hours or if I could see he needed it. One shouldn't keep reminding him to sit on the potty or asking him if he wants to go. And if he shows resistance of any kind then just pull his pants back up again.

*T*he mother of a not quite three-year-old girl told me her daughter refused to use the pot or the loo and would only wee in her nappy. She said that if the nappy was left off her daughter would hold on to her urine for four hours until her bladder was 'so full and painful' that her mother put the nappy back on. She told me that her daughter now thinks that doing a wee without a nappy on will hurt her. By asking her daughter all the time if she wanted to go the mother was magnifying a so-called problem. If nature wanted her daughter to go she would have to whether she wanted to or not.

I said how lucky her daughter was to have such a good bladder and that from now on she must put the nappies away in a cupboard and not ask her daughter all the time if she needs to go.

She should produce the pot after breakfast and if
her daughter doesn't want to sit on it then she
must say 'That's all right.' The child will then
eventually want to go and will either wet her
pants or say 'Nappy, nappy', at which the mother
must calmly say 'I've put the nappies away
because I thought you could sit on the pot to do
it and then we can pour it down the loo.' She
should keep light-hearted but insist. 'Oh dear, I'm
popping too. I'll sit on the loo and you can sit
next to me on the pot.' The mother must try not
to talk about it to anybody and stop asking her
daughter if she wants a wee – her daughter clearly has a very good quality bladder. Just keep the
pot available and possibly even leave her pants
off so she can wee when she feels like it.

Don't ask him all the time if he needs to go or you will
end up with a battle. Starting potty training later can be
a little more of a problem because children rebel. The
way they look at it it's a waste of time for them to sit
on a pot when they can just do it in their pants, but you
know your child well and if you realise he is just about
to do it you can quickly sit him on the pot and then say
'Well done, you've done it in the pot. We can now tip it
in the loo.' If this happens, quite often a child will
conform.

'Accidents' will happen

I would keep the whole thing very casual and expect a
few 'accidents'. I would certainly expect a child to
regress if he has learnt quickly. Practically all children
probably will change their mind again at some stage
and start doing it in their pants for a short time, but the

less you say and fuss about it, the quicker this period will be over.

If he says 'No'

If your two- or three-year-old says 'No' to the pot see how vehement he is. If he says 'No' to everything then I would just say 'Try it for a few minutes because I'll read you this new Sooty adventure.' Drag it out a bit longer and he probably will sit down whilst you read it to him. If he wants to look at it once he is off the pot then let him because he associates it with the pot and if the book is fun so will the pot be fun.

If he refuses to sit on the pot at all then, as with a younger child, just take the pot away and wait for three weeks before trying again.

CHAPTER SIX

How Diet Affects Your Child

WHEN I WAS A LITTLE GIRL CHILDREN WERE GIVEN syrup of figs once a week because a regular laxative was thought essential. I can quite clearly remember the advertisement: 'Mother, your child needs Syrup of Figs'.

We now know that normal, healthy children who have a good diet with plenty of fruit and vegetables don't really need laxatives and that it was just a foolish fad of the time.

What do I do about constipation?

There are children who really do have a constipation problem but they are few and far between and need medical attention, but on the whole children having a balanced diet with lots of fluid won't suffer from constipation. If your child is constipated for a few days, or you notice his stools are becoming like rabbit's droppings, then give them a little extra fresh fruit and vegetables, brown bread and other high-fibre foods to eat, such as a bran cereal, or extra water or fruit juice to drink but not a lot.

When to get medical advice

I certainly wouldn't give your child a laxative unless he has been constipated for three or four days and then I would simply increase those high fibre foods slightly as they are a mild, natural laxative. That should quite quickly make a difference, but if it does persist then you should seek medical advice. It's best not to worry, be guided by what your child seems to want to eat. On the whole if you offer your child a balanced diet then nature will tell him what he needs to eat and drink. A little girl I know does eat a great deal of fruit on a regular basis. Her body must need it.

If your child is constipated, just don't worry about it or talk about it, it won't do him any harm not going for two or three days. There are people who don't need to open their bowels every day. It depends on what your child normally does. And never put your child on the pot and leave him there 'until he does it'. That can cause more damage than the constipation.

A reason why your child might try to avoid opening his bowels could be that he has an anal fissure and so needs to be examined by a doctor. So if you have a child who normally has a bowel movement every day and then you notice he doesn't do much or anything at all for four or five days then I would take him to the doctor. It might hurt the child to empty his bowels.

If your child continually soils his pants, seek advice from your doctor as to why he does this because there may be something physically wrong (see also Chapter Seven, page 83). Don't talk about the child's problem in front of him.

How do I treat diarrhoea?

People use the word diarrhoea to mean the occasional loose stool, but this is not diarrhoea, it is quite normal and will have been caused by something that the child has eaten or drunk, like too much orange juice. I would ignore it unless it happens again. If there should be a loose, greenish-coloured stool watch out in case there are others or the child has a tummy ache as well. If the loose motion is accompanied by a tummy ache I would stop all dairy products, give the child warm boiled water to drink and a piece of dry toast if he is hungry – he probably wouldn't have much appetite anyway. It could have been caused by the child eating too many prunes or rather a lot of ripe plums or something similar. The next day he will probably be all right.

Diarrhoea is a condition and you will notice it because the child's stool has an extremely strong, unpleasant smell which is caused by an infection or by something that he has eaten which he should not have eaten. The stool will be extremely liquid and yellowish-greenish with mucus and possibly explosive and will be passed frequently. The child will feel quite unwell and won't want to eat so give his tummy a rest and just give him lots of fluids such as boiled water, and a rusk or a little dry toast if he wants anything. For small babies, glucose electrolyte drinks (like dioralyte) are recommended and if breastfeeding, it is important not to stop. If he is not better the next day then you must seek medical advice.

What if my child needs to wee a lot?

If your child is needing to urinate a lot it may be that he is cold, so keep his bottom well covered in winter. No doubt discarding a child's nappy for the first time may also make his bottom feel cold and cause him to urinate more often than usual. In the summer it is very often quite simply the result of children drinking a lot. When children are hot and thirsty they drink more and very often have to go to the loo more. An excess of orange juice will make the child urinate more and may also cause an irritation of the urinary tract.

If your child needs to urinate a great deal more than usual it is possible that he has a bladder infection and you should give him lots of water to drink and consult the doctor.

CHAPTER SEVEN

Will My Child Regress?

THERE MUST OCCASIONALLY BE A CHILD WHO DOESN'T regress, but I've never known one. Almost all children do so briefly, some once, some several times and it is very important to ignore it as it will not go on forever. It usually doesn't last for very long but it can happen again and again. Just keep going forwards, clean the child up and don't scold or it can turn into a problem.

Why do children regress?

Some children regress when there is some disruption in their lives, others regress after having used the pot quite happily and then they suddenly don't. It's almost as if they think 'Why am I doing it in here?' and then for a short while they do it in their pants. Soon they decide to use the pot again. One can't really work out what passes through their minds but it does happen.

Don't discuss and don't reward

Often it is the more intelligent children, two- to three-year-olds, who regress slightly at that stage. If your child rebels against the pot then just remove it with no recriminations whatsoever and no discussion and no rewards for going back on it. In three weeks reintroduce it and for the child who has been brought up with the pot in his life this stage will be easier. If he still rebels take it right away for another few weeks.

Putting a child on the pot early does not cause rebellion, but if your child is going to rebel (often these days aged even older than three because the pot is introduced so much later) and decides he doesn't want to sit on the pot, don't put his nappy back on, be prepared for a few days of mess. Just offer the pot casually when you see that he is bursting to go. If he doesn't want it, don't insist (see page 79).

The other thing besides disruption that may make a child regress even in a happy household is illness. If your child has a temperature he often reverts to an earlier stage, seems to become younger in various ways. Although his bowel movement may not be affected, he might well regress with his bladder control. A tired child might also wet his pants.

Children are individuals

All potty training problems stem from the personality of the person who is in charge. If you have a casual approach to the pot the child will gradually accept it, but an aggressive approach will result in a clash of personalities, a battle of wills because the child, like yourself, is an individual. All you will achieve in the child is uncertainty as to what is expected of him.

Whatever problem of regressing you have with your child, the most important thing is not to talk about it – either to the child or to anyone at all in front of the child. You may not think he will understand, but he will.

Don't make him feel guilty

The other thing you must never do is scold your child or make him feel guilty. I have heard of three-year-olds who have regressed and urinated on the floor being made to clean up after themselves. What a terrible thing to do – it would make the problem worse by making the child feel guilty and he'd wet more than ever and then be frightened of being told off and expected to clean up again. I wouldn't even say 'Don't dirty the floor' because it would be implying that you think his urine is dirty – it isn't. If your child has urinated on the floor it will be because for one reason or another he couldn't help it – his bladder needed to empty. If it happens again just mop it up and then wash the floor with a little disinfectant and change the child's pants. Don't make a fuss. Sometimes your child might even help you because he's seen you do it before. Just say 'Thank you. How kind.'

All the problems mentioned below will pass sooner or later, depending on the child's personality, on the age of the child and the individual problem itself. Most importantly it depends on the relationship of the parents to the child.

How long will it go on?

What a child achieves is what a child is capable of achieving, therefore a child chivvied into doing things better, quicker, who is unable to develop at the rate the parent is trying to develop him at is an unhappy child. Sometimes bowel and bladder control can't be achieved as quickly as you might hope it would be. Sometimes a week can seem like a year if you are waiting for your child to do something. Everything with child development can seem to take ages even though it is all over so quickly.

Just for your own interest and fun, put a cross in your diary when your child regresses and later when you look in your diary you will see that they actually only regressed for a few days (or weeks) a couple of times and you'll realise that you worried for nothing. Children cannot have bladder or bowel control before they are ready. It's Nature that does it, so sit them on the pot, but never get angry if they don't use it and if they do, well, jolly good.

When a child regresses

If the parent gives in and puts the child back into nappies simply to avoid soiled pants or wet bedding it is just spinning the problem out longer. Unless your child is absolutely hysterical, in which case you really have no choice, try not to go backwards in potty training – it just confuses the child who can't work out why one minute he hasn't got a nappy on and the next minute he has. The parents can't help being at their wits' end which reflects on the child who may feel that their distress is his fault.

It is important to remember that any problem will be very short term. No matter how much distress you and your child have gone through during this period, a few months after the event it will be completely forgotten. Your child will not be scarred for life over potty training problems.

My child will only urinate in a nappy

Several parents have contacted me with this problem. This usually happens once the child has been using a pot for a few months and then suddenly doesn't want to any more. Alternatively, it happens with children who have been introduced to the pot once they have bladder control and so can stand there with a full bladder demanding a nappy because it is familiar and in a way spells security.

Persevere with the pot

This problem occurs mainly in children from the age of two to three and a half. The last thing you want is a battlefield and in this situation, if your child is acutely distressed, I would be inclined to put the nappy back on for the short time needed as the child will be so relieved that the nappy is back. At the same time keep the pot in his sight and quite soon it will be sat on. It is very difficult to keep calm and not be angry but the situation should be handled in a very matter-of-fact way. If the child is determined to urinate in a nappy then in all fairness you should allow him to have it but persevere with the pot – always have it there. Each day the child develops in many, many ways and one day will use the pot. By the age of three and a half this problem will almost certainly be over.

My child will only poo in a nappy

Most of the parents who have asked me about this problem have children around the age of three and a half. Some are younger and I have come across it in a few four-year-olds but on the whole it is a three-year-old worry. Children who refuse to defecate except in a nappy are usually quite happy to urinate in their pot or in the lavatory. Once again, the last thing you want is a battle and, of course, if a child has always used a nappy he will be used to defecating in a standing-up position and so sitting on a loo or a pot will seem strange.

It seems to me that the parents of these children were always worried that it was dangerous for their child to hold on to his stools and so initially gave the child his nappy back too easily. It doesn't hurt a child not to defecate for a few days. On the whole if they have to go they will, unless you have punished them and they are afraid, in which case they will hold onto their stools when it really is necessary for them to do it. So if you can stay relaxed and not mind if you have 'accidents' for a few days or weeks, the situation will soon resolve itself.

This problem is based on fear. The child feels that he simply cannot do it anywhere else except in the nappy as that is where he has always done it. To expect him to change to a receptacle is very, very strange. The things you accept at one or two you query when you are older.

A father asked me what he should do about his three-and-a-half-year-old son who went to the loo quite happily by himself to urinate and slept without a nappy in the night, but when he needed to do 'Number Two' he asked for a nappy to be put on. He then ran about by himself until he felt like doing it into his nappy. They had tried putting him on the lavatory but gave up three days later as he still refused to use it. The problem had been going on for some months.

I suggested they should dispense with nappies altogether and not talk about them any more and beg friends and relations not to talk about the problem either. I said they should buy him a lavatory seat and a little stool and when he wanted his nappy they should very calmly say 'We're not going to do that any more. We've got this nice seat to fit on the loo, especially for you, and a thing to put your feet on so you're really comfy and you can do a Number Two in here instead of in a nappy.' (If he had already got a loo seat and stool I would buy him an extra large pot instead – something different.)

At the time he normally asked for a nappy or if he was getting a bit sniffy and looking a little uncomfortable, they should try and get there before him. 'I've got this nice pot for you instead of the nappy, you might find it more comfortable, and I've got a book that you might enjoy to look at whilst you're on the pot.' Then they should put him on the pot and hover around – not sit next to him, but be nearby and talk to him so the whole thing is rather cosy and friendly.

If after a very short time he stands up, they should say 'Oh, stay a bit longer. Give it a try because it is so much more comfortable in there than in your nappy.' If he rebels terribly and is desperately unhappy they will have to take him off the pot and just say 'All right, come on, let's put your pants back on.' He may then do it in his pants but they have to be prepared for that. They shouldn't put the nappy back on because, as he sees it, the nappy is for doing it in and if it's there it will take ages to get him out of defecating in the nappy.

At the same time they should start introducing more fibre into his diet so there is less likelihood of him getting constipated. They should expect accidents and should not be aggressive. It is very tiresome having to mop up a little bottom when it could so easily be avoided. Eventually it won't happen any more. At three and a half if they are calm but consistently firm the problem should not last much longer.

My child soils his pants

A mother once asked me about her six-year-old son who had soiled pants every night. I suggested she asked the doctor if there was anything physically wrong with her little boy as it is unusual for a child to be still soiling his pants at that age. Once the doctor had given him the 'all clear' I said she should just ignore the problem and it would go away.

Feeling threatened

Sometimes there has been an upheaval or disturbance in a child's life, such as a new baby who has reached eight months and become more of a threat, or starting school, possibly too young, or moving home. I think some children with this problem feel that defecation is a crime. Maybe they were once scolded for soiling their pants and so have started to hang on to their faeces. In all cases I first suggested seeking medical advice in case there was anything medically wrong. Once the parents knew there wasn't I suggested that the child should receive reassurance and understanding.

This problem is quite serious. If you have to cope with them you should examine your entire relationship with your child, and not just your relationship with regard to potty training, because your child obviously feels he must something in order to get your attention.

Listen, love and encourage

In all aspects of your child's life he should be listened to, given encouragement, shown love and appreciation. Even if you are tired and under stress in other areas of your life your child must get the idea that he is safe and loved. Quite often children do get shouted at and abused in the vain hope that it will change their behaviour; in fact they would rather be shouted at and abused than ignored. Make sure your children are listened to in all aspects of their life so they don't have to take such strong measures to make you take notice of them.

Some children soil their pants because of faecal incontinence caused by poor muscle tone in their bowel or anal sphincter (the muscle that enables the anus to contract). This is unlikely but possible and it would be as well to seek specialist advice to reassure yourself. The most likely reason your child is soiling his pants is chronic constipation (see Chapter Six). If this is the case your child will not be aware that he is soiling his pants. If he has not defecated properly for four days and has started soiling his pants then he may well have a problem and you should consult your doctor. You could also try changing his diet to include more roughage. Again, ignore the soiled pants, don't talk about them, just change them.

Attention-seeking ploys

This problem usually occurs among two- to four-year-old children, although there are incidences of much older children using their faeces and urine to gain attention. One of the usual ways of attracting attention is when a baby is being breast-fed. The toddler immediately wants to sit on the potty or go to the loo and, of course, it is a bit of a problem because if the request is ignored he might do it in his pants. Usually the older child doesn't need to go, he is just attention-seeking. This is irritating but you do have to respect it. I have known nannies who started the bottle feed by putting the toddler on the pot, but I would just keep the pot under the feeding chair as you can then produce it with one hand.

Very often as soon as you answer the telephone the child says he wants to go to the loo. All children do this, it is part of their development and starts because they cannot hear the voice at the other end of the receiver. Once a child is three I think you must explain to him in a relaxed way that he must be quiet when you are on the phone as otherwise you cannot hear the other person. It must become a general rule that you are not interrupted during any of them. Obviously you can cut short the call, but if your child hasn't mentioned it before the phone rang then you know he's probably not in any hurry.

Desperate to be noticed

A more serious problem is that of the child who uses measures such as smearing faeces on the sitting room walls, urinating on the bedroom floor or defecating in the garden. These are quite unhappy children who are desperate for attention. It is very sad because having done this anti-social thing they will be told off, but they are getting the attention that was their motive for such action in the first place.

I was once asked about three-and-a-half-year-old twins. The boy was quiet and gentle and the girl 'a bit of a handful'. Both were potty trained but the girl had started defecating in the garden and running away.

I said that I thought that the first time the little girl did this the parents must have got very, very angry which was a great pity as it ought to have been ignored. As it hadn't been ignored she knew that she could do it again to get attention. I suggested that if she did it again they should take no notice of it but started paying attention to her. Not cuddling and kissing her, but praising her both to herself and to others within her hearing.

If a child does anything 'antisocial' with their wees or poos the evidence should be swiftly cleared up and completely ignored.

My child wets his bed

A great many children wet their beds and the parents are in despair and think it will never go away. Occasionally it doesn't go away for a very, very long time, despite all the many 'remedies' suggested.

Normally when one is asleep and needs to empty the bladder, one comes to the surface, goes to the loo and then goes back to bed. But the true nocturnal enuresis, as it is known, is when people don't get the message to wake up and so the bladder empties itself into the bed.

In my experience children who wet their beds are usually highly sensitive children who need to sleep very deeply. I believe that their loss of control of the bladder is Nature's way of ensuring that they get the extra rest and relaxation that their personalities need. Once they get older and come to terms with life and are relaxed in the daytime they will wake up and go to the loo in the night when they need to. I don't think it can be cured. People suggest various bells and pads and things. These are well worth trying, if the child is willing, but I do know of cases where they didn't help at all – bells rang but the bed-wetters slept through. I think bed-wetters obviously can't help it.

I was once asked about a six-year-old girl who wet her bed once and sometimes twice nightly. Her mother had offered her nappies but she had refused them and didn't want to talk about her bed-wetting. Her parents had tried giving her gold stars for dry nights, restricting night-time fluids and potting before bed and again before midnight but nothing worked.

I thought this was very sad, the little girl

must have longed to have a gold star, but she couldn't win one because she couldn't help wetting her bed. She wished it didn't happen, but it did. I suggested that they shouldn't draw so much attention to it. Withholding drinks does, if anything, irritate the problem and putting the child on the pot in the middle of the night was just disturbing her and clearly not doing any good.

I was also amazed that the mother changed the child's bed. I would never have checked the bed to see if the child had urinated but would have left her to sleep peacefully. I would only change the sheets of a bed-wetting child if he woke up and was distressed. I think that if a child does wake up once he has urinated it is probably a sign that the problem won't go on for very much longer. Until then, as I explained to the little girl's mother, it is essential not to draw attention to the situation because her daughter is unable to control her bladder.

Wait for Nature's cure

Bed-wetting must never be talked about in front of the child or anyone else. You must certainly never make your child feel guilty by punishing him or talking about it. Don't withhold night time drinks if your child is bed-wetting as the bladder becomes irritated because the child hasn't taken enough fluid, thus causing the opposite effect. Do ask your doctor if there is anything medically wrong with the child and, if not, then I would wait until Nature cures it. Bed-wetting can also be inherited so ask your parents if there is a member of your family who once had, or who still has, the problem.

Don't talk about it

Until the age of eight some children wet their beds occasionally and I certainly wouldn't mention it or worry about it, but if once they got to eight and it was getting to be excessive – a wet bed every night – I would have a word with your doctor and ask them if you ought to seek advice. Before the age of eight it is a nuisance but nothing to worry about. Most of the parents who have contacted me regarding this problem have children between the ages of three and six. Some of the younger ones have started wetting their beds due to starting school too early or another major upheaval in their lives – often a nightmare causes a child to wet his bed. I have suggested that these parents do not put a nappy back on (and take it off if they have put it back on already) and do not talk about it and that it will be over in a maximum of six weeks.

If your child is invited to stay the night and he is a bed-wetter you must mention the fact to the mother and if necessary send a spare sheet and a rubber sheet. It is very, very likely that the child won't wet the bed in a strange house, possibly because he doesn't relax and sleep as deeply in a strange bed.

A note from Nanny

I do hope this book has helped to reassure you that what now seems such a problem will very soon be behind you. I'm quite sure there will be moments when you wonder if your child will ever be potty trained, but I assure you that this will happen – and all the sooner if you stop thinking of it as *your* problem and try to see the situation from your child's viewpoint. Then he will come to feel that you are on his side and will be more inclined to co-operate.

Don't let it upset you when everything seems to go wrong. Your anxiety will convey itself to your child and delay what you are trying to accomplish.

Follow my Golden Rules and keep as calm as you can. It is very difficult, I know, to keep calm when you are busy but you will soon have a child who no longer has wet or soiled pants.

Have confidence in yourself and your ability to cope. My way really does work if you follow it, so give it a fair trial.

Good luck!

Index